The Book of Birds

The Book of Birds

edited by
Penelope Layland
Lesley Lebkowicz

with artwork by
Fenja T. Ringl

The Book of Birds
Recent Work Press
Canberra, Australia

Copyright:
Poems © the authors, 2023
Artwork: © Fenja T. Ringl, 2023

ISBN: 9780645651379 (paperback)

A catalogue record for this book is available from the National Library of Australia

All rights reserved. This book is copyright. Except for private study, research, criticism or reviews as permitted under the Copyright Act, no part of this book may be reproduced, stored in a retrieval system, or transmitted in any form by any means without prior written permission. Enquiries should be addressed to the publisher.

Cover image: 'Spotted Pardalotes in Clematis' Fenja T Ringl, 2020.
Cover design: Recent Work Press
Set by Recent Work Press

Supported by

recentworkpress.com

Contents

SULPHUR

Ghazal for White Cockatoos	1
All the rusty hinges	2
Cockatoo evening	4
from arete	5
Thursday Morning	6

RAPTOR

The Eagle	9
Eagle	10
The eye	12

GANG-GANG

The gang	15
Raffish	16
Other ways	18

SWALLOW

Never	21
Salat al-maghrib	22
The Swallows Are Chasing	24

PIED

Before light, a magpie lark	27
Nest	30
#3 Naked Song	31
Butcher Birds, Mt Buffalo	32

COLOUR

King parrots' descent	37
Avian love knot	38

CHOOK

To My Neighbour's Hens	43
Hens	44

WATER

Eastern Curlew	49
Whooper swans (Iceland)	51
Pageantry	53
Gannet	56
Antarctic	57
Totem	58

LAND

Shooting the Bird	63
What the finch knows	66
'Pr-r-r-ew'	68
The Great Bowerbird	70
Kookaburra	72
Guinea Fowl	74
Megalong Valley	77

CITY

Roost	81
After a Painting by Tracey Moffatt	83
A bird at evening	84
Three pigeons	86
A Pair of Tawnies	87
Communion	90
The Plover on Campus	91
Epiphanies have wings	92

List of artworks	94
Acknowledgments	96
Contributor biographies	98

SULPHUR

Ghazal for White Cockatoos

Dotting morning trees like perky meringues a mob of white cockatoos
wake workers with their shark's cry of *White Cockatoos! White Cockatoos!*

Wheeling through the air from the wrong side of town, the bad boy & girl birds
bash trees, roar from Harleys under sulphur crested helmets badged *White Cockatoos.*

Sleep is murdered sure & dreams are polka-dot nightmares of kaleidoscope calls
as they rattle clouds, use trees as trampolines & chant the Rule of White Cockatoo.

Life is an orgy. Greedy claws and cheeky beaks snatch & grab from the orchard's
boring rows, each branch ruptured by Monsieur et Madame Connoisseur White Cockatoo.

Sheiks of the summer, their robes flow with more abandon than Lawrence of Arabia
could ever twirl on a train (& with more insight) just happy being a white cockatoo.

Heaven's Big Top, be it starched grey, circus stripe or panoramic blue, is the set
for our stars, Lords of Misrule, who sky-lark for poor us, who are not white cockatoos.

Earth needs these outriders, scouts at the edge of the black holed universe, warrior- clowns
who live long as humans (but upside-down). Disorderers of Australia, White Cockatoos.

At rest on a waving branch after another day's drama a second self emerges. Still as crystal,
sheathed like monks, they nod in contemplation, seeking the Way of the White Cockatoo.

I love them, my shadow self & totem, rejoicing each day in their cartoon drama,
and hope to rise like a phoenix to an afterlife flying and skiting with white cockatoos.

Ross Donlon

All the rusty hinges

All the rusty hinges in the sky creak open
and release clouds of
yellow-crested flying white.
This is heaven with no holds barred,
heaven claiming first place on the podium
and making sure we know about it,
pouring into and over every inch of sky
and branch and newly planted garden,
flapping and screaming and cavorting
to shred your other loves.

Lesley Lebkowicz

Lone Branch, 2022

Cockatoo evening

Look up!
        The cockatoos wing raucously about,
like surging white caps, that cross /
      recross
            the neighbourhood.

Raffish and rag-tag, purely out to enjoy themselves.
    Croaking their rude pleas
as they drag themselves about the sky in gay discord,
like tin cans tied behind the wedding car …

Until each, by wayward fits-and-turns
(in its own easy time,
according to personal whim, style and mood)
has eventually wended its way home.

To garage itself in its night haunt
in the dark pines by Hackett playing fields.

Paul Cliff

from arete

she would hear them approaching through the narrow corridor between her building and the one adjacent. a riot   a cacophony   a rage. the cockatoos had arrived for their swift visit to the giant fig tree that spread across the road. a daily tour of duty mimicking mocking the ships next to the naval base snaking the harbour nearby. the cockatoo opera. so wild so white in the premature new day. they swooped they circled they dived and swiftly disappeared. fractious ghosts. they excited her. dawn's vitamin. like the sound of waves crashing their foam onto a childhood shore.

joanne burns

Thursday Morning

the cockatoos
are raucousing the sky waves
battle front as a Reuter's
wire-rage from Iraq

in their wake
scattered heart-pit stones,
shredded flesh of fruit

Jennifer Kemarre Martiniello

RAPTOR

The Eagle

Sun haloes an eagle
diving to earth, her
crooked claws grab air,
then hook a rabbit
like a roc snatching
an elephant.
I want to be there one day
in the distant future, a spectre
floating above rice fields
a sudden vision glowing.
So let the eaglets
find a nest in my heart
to grow, safe from the dark
gravity beneath waves.
A slimy thing crawls
on the seabed, calls,
'Come die and live with me'.
Soaring, winds roar
& whistle above the clouds
where blue is thin air
—up here—and the Earth,
the sky is my gymnasium.

S. K. Kelen

Eagle

(New Year's Day, Quaama) (for M & S)

Your nest is a slovenly, couch-sized construct,
staggering in rudeness and power.
A Kontiki of sticks swept up by a vortex,
into the fork of a towering gum.
And more staggering still is the sight of you,
leaning out from it. Then pushing with great-socked feet,
to drop and momently impale yourself on air.
Before idly regathering—to swoop, long, steady and slow,
keeping limber and loose—
wheeling away in the direction of the sea.

Your heart equal in size to that which beats
in the rabbit-sized chest of the child
who bends to retrieve a foot-long feather
from the ferns. Then raises it overhead,
to jiggle its quill-point against the wash
of the blue, light-blasted sky.

Paul Cliff

Raven 2022

The eye

Once, inspecting the lambing paddock, strange
like a weathered root newly there, then closer,
I could say haughty but really, just staking its claim.
With one feathered trouser, it heraldic and refusing
to be intimidated, a wedgetail on a lamb. Its eye
held me till I left the paddock. Fair exchange.

Russell Erwin

GANG-GANG

The gang

The gang-gangs look like
they've slept in their feathers,
shabby-chic, stocky,
none of the parrot sleek.
Grey suits too baggy,
wispy hat-hair, bleary,
the dying, creaking croak
of a two-pack-a-day-er,
the munchies of a pot-head
in the hawthorn—
fuck, try these berries, man,
best berries ever,
I swear.

Penelope Layland

Raffish

Evolution had a bad hair day
the day it crafted you.
Trying for the Galah, some say,
but only part-way there by the shift's end,
and setting you aside on the workbench
to start anew.

Meantime, wily you,
inveigled yourself clean away.
But that's all spilt milk now.
And despite your undeniable shortcomings
and prototypic state—
poor finish and raggedy style;
your blighted, unkempt topknot,
untuned *grek-groke* call
and cockamamie, Marty-Feldman eye—
you're quite endearing (or at least compelling)
in your individual way.
We've grown attached to you,
and care for you as much as the galah
(some even *more*), today.
And are not averse to featuring you
in our *Big Book of Australian Birds* at all.

Paul Cliff

Raffish Neighbours, 2023 (detail)

Other ways

I keep his photo on my desktop and often open it:
he is beautiful: layered grey feathers rimmed
with white and settled in casual perfection;
the red mop top PL and PC have likened to the hair
of someone rising rumpled from their bed.
His eye holds mine, fearless, intimate,
my offering of seed at his feet and in his beak.
All these are wonderful but what draws me
is his gaze that says: there are other worlds and
other species and other ways of living.

Lesley Lebkowicz

SWALLOW

Never

Not a single swallow but the gulp
of them in the distance, banking
along the sunset, up cliff-
sides, brushing against
gilded fingertips
and gliding
back,

and it's not a single swallow but a swoop
of them, the whole diving towards
dusk, skimming the swimming
hole's surface and rising up
into the rafters
of night

it is never a single swallow but a richness,
cast like a net covering clouds,
then yanked towards earth,
moon crescent fastened
to pale morning
light.

Kimberly K. Williams

Salat al-maghrib

The evening call collides from minarets
and swallows drip from every age-pocked wall.
In twos and threes at first, from every fret,
then pulsing, flicker-black, with shrilling calls.

By hunger, habit, blood, they are drawn forth
to cling like bubbles then be cast adrift.
Wings slice the amber light in swoon and lift,
a choreography of swift and swift.

But swift is swift and prey is always prey.
From ground, the stringent ballet of the fly
—a grace-note to adorn a threnody—
is terrible: so small against the sky.

Penelope Layland

Welcome Swallows at Dusk, 2022 (detail)

The Swallows Are Chasing

And the swallows are chasing God
midair, skimming the green pools,
edging the cliffs. The swallows are
chasing God, building their nests
in the O of his name. The swallows
are chasing God, and we must chase
the swallows as far as our flat feet
and wingless backs will allow: around
the fat cottonwood, over the gravel,
across the bridge that spans El Rito,
past the Bear Spotted Here notice, down
to the tip of the massive ruby sky.

Kimberly K. Williams

PIED

Before light, a magpie lark

A sound, a couple of sounds and a perforation
of the dark when there is no hour, a voice probing,
in the way a child calls out. Anxious, it diminishes
as soon as it calls. Is absorbed in the dark's smother.

Chill notes, harsh, brittle, they're not enough
to unravel or flute into ribbons and arias.
Neither is there a flood or generosity in it.
There is a song but not singing. Not sweet either.
The ripeness of a grey shrike-thrush's lyric
tops it like a cello gracing us from another garden.
Or the liquidity of currawongs indulging fugues of fabulous sorrow.

It is plaintive, lost. This thin voice
is the simple truth of this place:
It speaks of sticks, of noon, of distance,
of no others near. "No-one here, here."
Wincing like an axe worked free,
it carries over the years, from Villawood
and a school playground, 1960s. Always,
further off, and further.
Or a Saturday afternoon, a small voice,
somewhere in the expanse of a car-park.
In the new subdivision
it cries through those gums left standing.
And in the moment it ceases

that emptiness, that waste of hours.
This is Radio Australia relayed from the heart.
It is a self, a continent seeking consolation.
At this hour though, this is far from certain.
I listen. It stops. And it is lost to the dark.

Russell Erwin

Magpie "Pesky", 2014

Nest

In bare branches of the jacaranda tree
two peewees settle and flutter
around the dark cup of their nest
(Are there babies?
It's too hard to see from down here
on the verandah of my parents' house)
the mother bird huddles down cosily
in her tiny home ...
unaware of rustling pages
and the scraping of a chair
on wooden floorboards
as my father reads and remembers
in soft rays of lonely sunshine ...

Anita Patel

#3 Naked Song

(2016)

My mother was a Currawong
with sleek black feathers
trimmed with white
and a beak that broke down bones, cracked through lizard hide
pointed the way through mazed tree tops and curved snarling down at the corners.

She kept her yellow eyes closed in hours of darkness to preserve their colour;
sharpened them on everything I did in the daylight. When she sang her voice was ringing

setting the sun just so or calling up morning
with the single swoop to song, cadence almost finished – but not quite.

Her own naked name, over and over
until to hear it meant nothing:
and that was her tragedy.

Lucy Alexander

Butcher Birds, Mt Buffalo

Grey and black, yellow-eyed, thick-shouldered,
scuffing up dust in mugging pairs around the camp:
each squared-off leafy site beneath its brittle stretch
of alpine ash their gamblers' patch that spits up
sticks and bread and crackers at a kick,
sausage-nubs and old bent chop bones,
anything to take their minds from rodents
and the screeches of their bratty nested young.

All grey and grey-black inside as well as out,
their ganged-up shoulders unshrug to wings
that loop them up into their other selves
where alpine ash whisper to them in a blue high tone
about the shaking weight of mountain seasons
moving through them blind and ravenous as angels.

Kevin Brophy

White-winged Chough, 2015

COLOUR

King parrots' descent

In Spring's sweet motorcade, the three fruit trees—
apple, apricot and pear—arrayed at our back fence
have dropped their crimson-white flowers
like tickertape … As a King parrot pair,
leaving off the chiacking and malarkey
of their high-wire shenanigans, swing down
onto the apple's upper branch. Face off from its opposite ends,
then ape-walk toward each other, fist-over-beak-over-hand,
to meet and playfully bump heads.
Brazenly canoodle there, in their savage, spraycan orange
and two-tone green.
Their cries—two taut-and-perfect pealing bells—
cutting my tame-and-flabby heart like razor-wire
to its core's quick.

Paul Cliff

Avian love knot

The galahs arrive in pairs and perch
on the rim of the feeder, taking turns to bob their heads

to the grain. Sometimes they turn towards each other,
one higher and curving down, the other below

and angled to face upwards, creating a loose avian love knot.
There's a sculpture of them in this pose in Watson,

near the Highway. They're famous for fidelity,
paragons of passion—for each other, majestic

and magisterial in monogamy. This is how
they live from the time they get together

until one dies. Isn't this what we all want:
this harmony, this trust?

Lesley Lebkowicz

Flame Robin, 2022

CHOOK

To My Neighbour's Hens

Clara and Claudia, I hope you always stare
at nothing in particular, taking turns through the garden
savouring angelica, borage, and thyme. I hope you
always gussy up your tail-feathers towards a proud
Rock Cornish rooster who has a rubicund comb,
a deep-burnished chest and an oratorical voice.
May you always scratch at the earth among
the ordinary sounds of tree branches swaying,
dogs barking, leaves blowing, and never have
to live on a sloping wire floor with six other birds
in a space the size of a filing cabinet drawer,
your beaks cut off, all of you starved, bald,
mad, never seeing daylight. May your male chicks
never be snatched away from you and put through
a high-speed grinder, mixed with hormones
and fed to you, making you grow faster than your bodies
can cope with before you are trucked off to slaughter,
the sky cracking inwards like an egg. May you
always walk through yard-light and the rain's grainy
footage and sleep on butter-coloured straw
where you watch tufts of your down drift
through sun shafts, knowing nothing about battery
cages, the jets of water that scald away
feathers, or the motorised blades that slit throats.
May you always be fed corn, oatmeal, spaghetti,
chow mien and risotto left-overs, the crusts
of toast and dark pumpernickel, green and yellow
kitchen scraps into which genial, attentive humans
have mixed the shells of your own good eggs.

Judith Beveridge

Hens

I think I've been waiting for you all my life.
To glimpse you through the kitchen window
scratching between iris and daffodil,
disrupting roots, sprawling moll-like
in a patch of sun, wings spread flush
with the ground, a coquettish leg
in the air and rolling lascivious eye.
You're disruptive of course—
annuals, seedlings go by the wayside,
Christmas lilies cordoned off,
brassicas like khaki interns on parade—
but what small price
for that vigorous rustling
as mulch scatters from under hedges,
to have you beady at my side
grabbing worms as I pull up buttercups;
or whetting your beaks on the path, this side
that side, like good chefs sharpening knives.
I love the way you pose like weathervanes
on the axe handle,
to watch as I wash dishes
how today's menu, or tonic
is borage or bindweed or dock
that you will strip back
to a handful of cellulose spikes.
The way you share a laying box
when there is one for each of you
and midwife one another
through your confinements.

The way you lay eggs—
those warm white ellipses
on the straw.
Somehow for all the wreckage
the garden was never more alive.
You offer a remote conviviality
that I don't presume upon
as I would, say, a dog or cat,
I'm afraid it's species that I'm celebrating here,
not personality,
that atavistic sense of well-being you provoke
you unremarkably remarkable hens.
I'm grateful, watching you just now
splashing about in dust
for that reassurance you give,
of simple notions, like goodness.

Sarah Day

WATER

Eastern Curlew

A contagion like telepathy
ruffles the flock
shuddering with altered light
and wind, a pectoral yearning
for the dot to dot of stars
and the mind's magnet drawn
to the Arctic. We lift,
we float and feather and fan
back to Earth. And lift and float again
our slow rehearsal on the shore.
Some call it *Zugunruhe*—
this restlessness to move—our lust-
longing for the breeding grounds
of Russia, China and Siberia.
We've done with mud dibbling
day and night, dispensed for now
with lagoon and sand flat months,
the serenity of sea grass.
We're leaving at nightfall,
the long haul North calls.
No one has signalled
yet we are all of one mind
and we are rehearsing:
lifting, fanning, floating,
chatting about anything but
the Journey and the Gobi Desert gold
of the Yellow Sea halfway
glinting and shrinking—
no longer crab rich in bog and marsh,

more road and wall now and human
tower, putrid leaks and pestilence.
We curlews fossick clean sand,
we probe salt clean mud
for limpid life, we are not
sludge siphons, and the psychedelia
of plastic bits that lure the eye
twists the guts. Some friends turn back,
resolved to make Summer of Winter,
others will slacken from the flyway
with hunger over a dark sea.
Pulled by memory, hope,
and this deep ancestral ache
the rest of us who leave
this ancient continent tonight
will set our compass
for Kamchatka, Amur …

Sarah Day

Whooper swans (Iceland)

no swans on Avon, these,
scudding by mild, lawn-edged banks

these are distant
scant white patches
huddling down on the
　stark edge of an empty inlet.

pressed in close to the dark-mossed rocks
they are trying to be
small blank resting spaces
　outside the wind's fretting

spare white hyphens
punctuating the black water
—too many to count
—too far off to see
　that their feathers are ruffling

their rubber legs treading
the waters of a flinty bay
chill enough to burn
　anything else less fierce away.

they have travelled far
to congregate here, less like
immigrants – out of desperation
than feathery pilgrims, homing in
　to the land of their swan-fathers

breasting the air-gusts
paddling the cold swan roads
tracking the pristine conditions
 for regeneration

because only the ice can
colour their wings bright
and this black water the strong beaks
 of their progeny.

Jean Page

Pageantry

A still spring morning on the beach,
for the first time in days, no breeze,
the water in the bay flat calm, I was
thinking as I walked of the millions
of tiny shells that crunched beneath
my feet, the filigree intricacy
of their design, such delicate
homes: how much abundant life
is hidden from us. I allowed my gaze
to rise and look out to sea,
the ragged line of the mountains
misty against the blue. It was then
I saw them, five black swans
 in effortless cruise, single file flotilla,
their slow elegance a demonstration
of all we are not, a contrast to
flagged warships or vain parades
with blaring brass and banging drum,
displays of power which suggest
how insecure we feel our place here,
how needy the quest to make certain
our uncertain home. The swans
continued serene in their element.
One lifted a great wing. I saw the flash
of white feathers on the underside,
a shock of surprise. It was as if
for a moment I saw both creature

and angel and knew I was a stranger
to their habitations, yet recognised
in the certain glide, the hidden paddle
something of majesty, an inhuman
guide to wild revelation.

Adrian Caesar

Little Pied Cormorant, 2023

Gannet

Call us experts
of mathematical precision,
of motion parallax
and high-speed depth perception.
Admire the vatic eye inside
Egyptian kohl lined hieroglyphs.
Construct all the models you will
to test how an observer
might form a view of the world
at one location
yet use it at another.

And I will say how hunger fills a gap
when time stops in a breathless
break-neck streamlined plunge;
that the thrill of breaking
through water from air
is a conversion of mind and body
and that a snared fish, silver in the bill,
is a new idea of heaven, every time.

Sarah Day

Antarctic

The horizon of the albatross is not fixed,
as that of the landbird,
into a settled, navigable matrix.
Mountains vulcanise each ash-grey moment
and crumble in foam and thunder.
The caldera yawns, wet as jaws,
Then blinks black, blandly opaque.
The air too is alpine, solid with stress:
peaks bulge and peter beneath
pivoting, fingering wings.
Surviving such tumult means seeking no harbour,
expecting no succour,
giving weight fully to the wind.

Penelope Layland

Totem

I

Amid the merry junk and bric-a-brac
in the tourist village gift-shop
a chart purports to show by birth date
my Native American totem creature.

I'm with my wife, daughter, grand-girls.
We're having fun. They are delighted
not vindictive, as they cry, You're a goose.
Silly needs no saying.

I join in laughter, see the round-hulled body
the too short legs, long craning neck,
sharp featured beak, the ungainly waddle,
all my clumsiness.

But then I remember wild migrations
with sure compass and deliberation
in strict formation, the pink-footed geese,
every year their elegant resolve in flight.

II

A brutal time of loss
driving from the nursing home
in an English autumn of dark mourning
towards the old place I was clearing for sale
my father dead, my mother immobile
fogged in delusion, hallucination,
against a darkening sky, I saw

                                                                          grey geese
                        head of
        an arrow   full of   fast   purpose
                        in their
                                                          certain flight.

Every year they land in fields that surround
the industrial decay of the suffering town
on their way to feed at Martin Mere
before their onward journey south
away from the vast freeze of Iceland.

                                        I can't say how or why the sight
                                      filled me with strange exultation
                                      as if I soared with them carried by the
                                      vast energy of their wingbeats.

```
                              migration
                my own
It made         from home     to home
                seem less
                              unnatural
```

        Looking backwards there was also looking
forward, the possibility of charting a course
to let my task of grief become winged fuel
speeding me through the dark and lowering
passages towards a resting place
in warmth and light.

Adrian Caesar

LAND

Shooting the Bird

Was it there when the scrub-bird raked the gully
and sang with the crickets and the barking dog;
was it there in the laughter of farm-boys,
when each implement of an army knife dragged

across a phalarope's breast? When you surveyed
your paddocks and the wind chanted a campfire
song about a billabong ghost—was it there;
or could it be heard in the snip of the bale-breaker

across the ears of your fly-blown sheep; or in
the spanner music of your Saturday drives?
Uncle, when you primed the pump to the pant
of your cattle-dog's thirst, when you scattered

starlings from the backs of Holsteins; when you put
the chilled mouthpiece of dusk to your lips
and unsettled galahs from their trees and crows
from fenceposts and hawks from the sky above

the watercourse, was it there cawing from a branch
out of which not even the kestrel would swoop?
Uncle, you never told us the name of the bird that flew
into your head and made a habitat of the scrub-dark

flat horizon the other birds returned from.
You never told us, looking up into the eucalypts,
if it was the dove or the pigeon gone to ground;
or the warbler who sings with a split pitch;

or if it was the bird Mitchell heard and perhaps
Sturt when he was lost; or if it was the bird
that sang to Leichhardt and called his flying spirit
to the dust. You never told us if it was the egret

that sat on the wreck of its ribs and swallowed
its cries; or if it was the falcon whose talons
and tail-feathers clung to the wire. Uncle,
I've my own theory: that it was one of those birds

that soar over the mountains from Gundawarra Shire,
that shift weight and cry then bank back towards
the Divide; a bird with a wingtip blue as a tarn,
wide as an inland lake. Though the way you took

to your rifle to shatter those cries made me think
perhaps it was a bird that never came so far
but stayed near inlets and tried its music round
the coves. But Uncle, when the barn owl

plummeted the crevasse; when the hornets built nests
in the marram; when the mealy-bugs ate the winter
sorghum and the nuptial flights of termites
headed for the slap-board shack; when the bushfires

called us out to listen if it was the oriole's
or the thrush's burnt cry over the house—I'm certain
each of us heard it. And sometimes when a fieldmouse
fell from the talons of a goshawk into the Barwon,

when the pratincoles lifted from their clay-pan
as if they'd decided to live and die on the Barrington Tops—
I'm sure I heard it. But Uncle, when you took down
your rifle and the bullet found its groove

and the barrel that disquieting branch, we didn't hear
what adverse wind or current brought the cry of a bird
to slaughter on a far-off gibber steppe. Uncle,
I'm still looking for some evidence. And we never

found out if it was the bird that just wanted to lift
its wings and search for honey in the rock. Before
you fired, you laid down these two rules: read the
weather-maps and keep the sun behind you as you look.

Judith Beveridge

What the finch knows

The finch knows mainly one thing:
Its joy is full of it, body aquiver

with sensible fears of what today
might slide shadowy over it.

The finch knows to keep each eye
on each side of its world

as it splashes in a roadside puddle
of light and sand and broken water.

The finch knows mainly this one thing.
Its love is full of it. It fills trees

with twisting flight. The finch plays close
to others out of fearful love

and disappears into leafy worlds
when the near wind hisses

like a cruel husband frightening
his latest wife. The finch is loved

for being small, bright, neat, fast.
It knows every seed and spring

in every wrinkle of its fearful songful world.
The finch knows how to live

in joyful fright and fret, knows
every shadow in every corner of its world.

Kevin Brophy

'Pr-r-r-ew'

My son when small, carried a stick,
scything it about and shouting
syllables martial-heavy
as he entered a paddock
tall with rank phalaris
so not to be frightened
when quail burst,
small land mines,
like messages from the future
exploding at his feet.

Russell Erwin

Superb fairy-wren, 2021

The Great Bowerbird

I have all the white things.
I have gathered them here, together.
In this place of stone, rust, sky and ochre
even at dusk they glow.

I have the sharp-edged chips of quartz,
the bleached spiral shells
long empty of their juicy morsels.
I have this bone set with gleaming teeth
which I have laid out apart from the rest.
It holds its own.

When it catches your eye
you will see this pale apron splayed
in invitation, a stage reaching out
from my finely thatched sanctuary
where more pale prizes
glimmer in the shade.

I have eaten, and preened.
I feel the magenta crest
bloom on my neck. It is time to parade
with jutted tail, stiff wings and plume.
To croon and lure you for an instant
of congress. Then we part forever.

May you lay and raise
new generations
to perpetuate
my resplendence.

Jacqui Malins

Kookaburra

All night I hear the comedy
of your grief; the lynched note,
the manic lyric; your cheering

self-throttling riff of grief.
There is sobbed cackle, panicked
hilarity when you stretch your

fretted neck to the plectrum
of a dry leaf. No lyrebird's
pickpocket throat could turn

your tragic joke; a high-heeled
descant down then up a stair.
Is it laughter Kafka could invent,

Accompaniment to a grandiloquent
event? Oh bird, who can mimic
my keening note? I know what

touches us all with its simple
vote. Oh yes, you seem to quip,
death is life at its most burlesque.

Judith Beveridge

Regent Honeyeater in Grevillea, 2020

Guinea Fowl

With a quail-shaped body
and a vulture-like head
they look like crossbred turkeys
or blue-ribbon hybrid hens.
Though in the kingdom of birds
this seemingly assorted
mixed bag is an independent flock
who, in slate-dark plumage
and moony-bright spots,
quills that a milliner would crave,
scratch around like Miss Marple,
stealthy as barnyard cats.
Nimble-footed in stifling
frocks, shrewd and anti-social,
they scour the land like ducks on water
but are nowhere near as quaint.
And they're far too busy
to swan about in a peacock suit
with the air of a lark ascending.
Theirs is the head down
hard-nosed blitz of unruly order,
driven as if by recompense or dutiful need.
In a gregarious grey-cloud tumbleweed
tight-knit pack, they've come to rid
the paddocks of seasonal peril:
locusts, spiders, ticks
and old bald-faced misery.
Together they're in their element,
relentlessly rummaging,

constantly bending and pecking,
rooted to the spot at hand
in fastidious delight.
They do not care for the manacles
of a bygone world: kingdoms
of a fallen age, empires in the dust.
It's the sovereign dirt beneath their feet
and the babble of whistling chirps,
the workaday nod and lacing of beaks
that sets them apart from the hunt
in the grass.
          As for the snake—
out from its pit of a hollowed log,
uncoiled as the rays of the sun,
needling through the underbrush
like a thick plait rivering in swards of green,
craving, I suppose, to slither head-on
into the banquet of the henhouse floor—
morning has lured it into the open,
freed it from the nocturnal swoop
of an owl and the hunt of a ravenous fox.
And as dawn unfurls in swathes
of random order, cold-blooded
with earthly hunger the snake
slides-on, red tongue hissing,
a slick of fire across the feral sprawl.
Though in the eye of the guineas
it's merely a link in the chain of pests.
They'll spot one wriggling
in the burning distance or coldly
stalking under hot-flushed straw.
Then one by one they band together,

surround it in encircling ranks,
and with machinery screeches
they scourge in a cross-fire attack,
butchering it from head to tail
until the snake lies twitching
like a severed limb. And through
the punctured scales of its deathly skin,
in holes where there once were eyes,
they riddle it over with jackhammering pecks
leaving nothing more than a plaything,
bones for the driveling wind.

Todd Turner

Megalong Valley

The gods banned machines from ever
entering the last pure tract of Megalong.
Here, even bracken's picturesque
& the whipbird, breathless
with the beauty of it all,
is silent, reverential.
There's a waterfall
splashing a rainbow
you walk under
that's always there and will be
until the earth or sun shifts
sandstone cliffs, a kookaburra
laughs from gorgeous gloom
up & down, up & down.

S. K. Kelen

CITY

Roost

He settles at the table
Pale eyes, baleful
DAAAAAHN'T, DAAAAAHN'T
he cries, when pressed
for any explanation

These ones come home too,
you know—these furtive ravens
This one here will home
and home, he will nest
with his rusted panel van

in your front yard, fag packets
strewing the lawn   His familiar,
the blue cattle dog, will howl
and howl, enacting this long
tethering, a collar of old rope

lashed to wheel-less axle
You had thought that,
fledged, he would fly
and fly   He was equipped
only to dumpster-dive

and boomerang   He settles
at the table, plumage dark
and greasy   Scrapes his chair
Nips another fag from the packet
with thin fingers, spreads his

awkward shoulders, coughs
Refused a light, he shudders;
huffs   *FAAAAHHHHK YOU*
The pale eyes leak   He glares
and glares, and slumps, stropping
his beak   on your peace

Melinda Smith

After a Painting by Tracey Moffatt

she's dancing
with crows
the dream
blurring black winged
out of the colonial
nightmare
poised
on the brink of earth
in the tattered silks
of the desired
hair
whipped to black
feathers
wild wind dancing
with crows
lifting from the brink
of rock
into the storm
stained sky she dances
dances the crows
dances the dream
dances the storm
pink sky

Jennifer Kemarre Martiniello

A bird at evening

That bird outside knows something
with its evening cry, first long and short,

the following notes falling, trilling, long,
the day's goodbye: what others, feeling melancholy,

might call mournful. I say, summing up the day's
work, jotting on the diary of the air.

Today I found two carcasses of birds along the path,
one old, the other very young. The common warbler.

What the bird's song says is here is something
to fill nothing, that cannot stay empty long.

Poems say this also. What the bird and I collect
is each day's emptiness. We give it back,

when things fall silent, start again, as if the
failure of each day is all we know, is all our art.

Michael Sharkey

Afternoon Protest, 2022 (detail)

Three pigeons

I watch three pigeons stutter-strutting the vacant lot
    next to the repurposed church in the Inner West.
One follows another who mirrors the first. Is it
    habit or superstition that makes something
circular of this triangular claque of wings, like
    oil on seawater throwing colours off its
bobbling surface, rolling from a purple sheen to
    green and back again? Sometimes days like these fly
into my eye, an exclamation of multitasking
    sunshine marshalling the bright walls. One pigeon
hops, another spreads his wings carnally, and like
    the third way in an argument, the last one ebbs
and pecks, but can't evade the revolving syllogism
    of their walk. A screen without edges bathes us
in its blue: those aren't clouds, but systems
    shepherding the day across the sky.

David Musgrave

A Pair of Tawnies

6:30 on these August mornings
I've only slowly come to see
a pair of tawny frogmouths who
have learned to imitate the tree

they've roosted on for generations
before we human beings arrived,
brandishing new names for them
according to our several tribes.

Have the tawnies huddled there
ever heard their name in Latin?
Podargus strigoides. Yes,
taxonomy inflicts its pattern.

They seem so paired and unassuming
dozing on their winter branch,
back from one long night of killing
frogs and slugs and mice and ants.

I'd rather hoped they'd glide like owls
romantic on the midnight air
but though I'm told their flying's 'weak'
there's little that evades their stare.

Some mornings they do not appear.
Do they choose another tree?
Why is it when they're not at home
we feel our own fragility?

Geoff Page

Tawny Frogmouths, 2012

Communion

After Helen Macdonald's essay, 'Nests' (in Vesper Flights)

She shifts inside the tightening shell,
aligns herself for flight, beak pointed
to where light filters in. Then feels
the warmth of hands around her shell
and hears a soft sound yearning –
and replies, not as an almost hatching bird
to something not-bird, but voice to voice,
one responding to another with the same urge.

All this is heard and understood
by bird and human.
Not bound by species, the feeling flies
from one life to another, found by chance,
by circumstance,
by something more than luck.

Lesley Lebkowicz

The Plover on Campus

She ran out in front of us like a mother
with a flat tyre trying to flag down help
from the side of the road. The man's English
kept cracking like a stick broken into
several uneven pieces: *Cambodia kill
so. Many. Life here. Good. Mother.* He
points to the loud plover, who like a kill-
deer attempts to distract us from her chick.
See? Mother protect baby. Yes, I nod.
*Cambodia worse for women 100%. Some
men not nice. Too cold for baby.* He points.
See mother make warm. Here. Birds. Free.

Kimberly K. Williams

Epiphanies have wings

Chase them
like a child
chases seagulls.
Or stay still,
be quiet.

If you are engrossed
in what intrigues you
about the world
and how to live in it
one might come closer,
curious.

Don't look,
even from
the corner
of your eye,
even if one
squawks for
your attention.

If it is your epiphany,
it will only swoop
when it knows
you are ready,
put its fat hot chip
right into
your hand.

Jacqui Malins

Spotted Pardalotes in Clematis, 2020

List of artworks

All artworks by Fenja T. Ringl, a Canberra artist who takes inspiration from the patterns and details found in Australia's fascinating nature and ecosystems to create hand printed and layered artworks on paper and on porcelain.

page			
3	Sulphur crested cockatoo	*Lone Branch*, 2022, drypoint	14.8 x 20 cm
11	Raven	*Raven*, 2022, linocut and monotype	15 x 10.5 cm
17	Gang-gangs	*Raffish Neighbours*, 2023 (detail), 2023, linocut and drypoint (hand-coloured)	28 x 40 cm
23	Swallows	*Welcome Swallows at Dusk*, 2022 (detail), drypoint	34.7 x 21.7 cm
29	Magpie	*Magpie "Pesky"*, 2014, linocut and monotype	15 x 10.5 cm
33	White-winged chough	*White-winged Chough*, 2015, linocut (hand-coloured)	13.5 x 9 cm
39	Flame robin	*Flame Robin*, 2022, linocut (hand-coloured)	12 x 17 cm
55	Little pied cormorant	*Little Pied Cormorant*, 2023, solar plate etching	8.9 x 6.9 cm
69	Superb fairy-wren	*Superb fairy-wren*, 2021, linocut and monotype (hand-coloured)	90 x 21 cm

page			
73	Regent honeyeater	*Regent Honeyeater in Grevillea*, 2020, linocut and solar plate etching (hand-coloured)	21 x 29.5 cm
85	Silver eye	*Afternoon Protest*, 2022 (detail), linocut and monotype (hand-coloured)	20 x 35.5cm
89	Tawny frogmouth	*Tawny Frogmouths*, 2012, linocut (hand-coloured)	22 x 15 cm
93	Spotted pardalote	*Spotted Pardalotes in Clematis*, 2020, linocut and solar plate etching (hand-coloured)	21 x 29.7 cm

Acknowledgments

The Book of Birds would not have been possible without the support of the ACT Government, through a generous grant awarded in the 2023 Arts Activities funding round.

'Ghazal for White Cockatoos' was published in *Lucidity* (Mark Time Books, 2017).

'Never' and 'The swallows are chasing' were published in *Still Lives* (Gazebo Books Life before Man imprint 2022) and 'The swallows are chasing' was shortlisted for the University of Canberra International Poetry Prize 2019

'Raffish' (published as 'Gang-gang') and 'King parrots' descent' were first published in *Canberra Light* (Recent Work Press 2019)

'Cockatoo Evening' was shortlisted for Poetry in ACTion (2007) and was published in *Canberra Light* (Recent Work Press 2019)

'Antarctic' was first published in *The Canberra Times* in 2020

'A bird at evening' was published in *The Foliage in the Underworld* (Puncher & Wattmann 2018)

'Eastern Curlew' was commissioned by Bett Gallery's Poets & Painters project and was part of a collaborative artwork with printer Raymond Arnold. It was published in *Towards Light* (Puncher and Wattman 2018). Also published in *Towards Light* was 'Gannet'

'Hens' was published in *The Ship* (Brandl and Schlesinger 2004)

'Roost' was published in *Man-handled* (Recent Work Press 2019)

'Butcher birds, Mt Buffalo' and 'What the finch knows' were published in *In This Part of the World* (Melbourne Poets Union Inc 2020

'Shooting the bird' was published in *Accidental Grace* (UQP 1996), as was 'Kookaburra'.

'To my neighbour's hens' was published in *Sun Music: New and Selected Poems* (Giramondo 2018)

'Nest' was published in *A Common Garment* (Recent Work Press 2019)

'Guinea Fowl' first appeared in *Connective Tissue, Newcastle Poetry Prize Anthology 2015*, (eds Judith Beveridge and Robert Gray) and then in *Thorn* (Puncher and Wattmann, 2020).

Contributor biographies

Lucy Alexander is a poet and resident of Ainslie+Gorman Arts Centre. *Strokes of Light* (Recent Work Press, 2020) was her third collection of poetry. Her work is widely published in journals. She received the CAPO Cook Creative writing prize as well as being shortlisted for the International Prose Poetry Prize, 2022.

Judith Beveridge is the author of seven collections of poetry, most recently *Sun Music: New and Selected Poems* (Giramondo, 2018), which won the 2019 Prime Minister's poetry prize. She has taught poetry in schools and Universities and in the public domain and was poetry editor for 'Meanjn' 2005-2015. She lives in Sydney.

Kevin Brophy's latest book is the short story collection, *The Lion in Love* (Finlay Lloyd, 2022).

joanne burns is a Sydney poet. She is currently assembling a new collection of work, *rummage*. She has been active in the Australian poetry scene since the early 1970s.

Adrian Caesar is the author of 12 books including poetry, fiction, and non-fiction. He was born in the UK but has lived and worked in Australia for 40 years. His latest publications are *This Cathedral Grief* (Recent Work Press, 2020) and a novel, *A Winter Sowing*, (Arcadia/ASP, 2021).

Paul Cliff is a Canberra-based writer. His most recent collections are *A Constellation of Abnormalities* (Puncher & Wattmann, 2017) and *Canberra Light* (Recent Work Press, 2019).

Sarah Day's ninth book is *Slack Tide* (Pitt Street Poetry, 2022). Her books have won awards including the Queensland Premier's, Wesley Michel Wright and the Anne Elder Award and been shortlisted for the Prime Minister's, Tasmanian, and NSW Premier's Awards.

Ross Donlon has published five books of poetry, the latest being *The Bread Horse* (Flying Islands, 2020) and *For the Record* (Recent Work Press, 2021). Winner of two international poetry competitions and other awards, he has read his poems in many parts of Australia, the U.K. & Europe. Born in Sydney, he now lives in Castlemaine, Victoria, where he convenes poetry readings and is publisher of Mark Time Books.

Russell Erwin is a farmer in the Southern Tablelands whose life there allows him the opportunity to observe the life of birds appearing in these poems.

S. K. Kelen has been writing poems for longer than he cares to remember. He enjoys sports, travel, gardening on cool sunny days and hanging around the house, philosophically. His most recent books are *A Happening in Hades* (Puncher & Wattmann, Waratah; 2020) and *Love's Philosophy* (Gazebo Books/Life Before Man, Summer Hill; 2020).

Penelope Layland is a poet and editor. Her most recent book, *Beloved* (Recent Work Press, 2022), was a winner in the ACT Notable Book Awards.

Lesley Lebkowicz's most recent book is *Mountain Lion* (Pitt Street Poetry, 2019). *The Book of Birds* is her first as co-editor of an anthology.

Jacqui Malins is a multidisciplinary artist and poet, living and working on the lands of the Ngunnawal and Ngambri people, in Canberra. Her first poetry collection, *F-Words*, was published in 2021 (Recent Work Press). Find Jacqui and her work on stage and page, in galleries and online at www.jacquimalinsart.com.

Jennifer Kemarre Martiniello OAM is a writer and visual artist of Aboriginal, Chinese and Anglo-Celtic descent. Her books include *The Imprint of Infinity* (Tidbinbilla Press), *Black Lives Rainbow Visions*, *Writing Us Mob* and *Talking Ink from Ochre*, (all Aberrant Genotype Press). Literary awards she has received include the Henry Lawson Literary Award, the Canberra Critics Circle Award for Literature and the Banjo Paterson Poetry Prize.

David Musgrave's most recent collection is *Selected Poems* (Eyewear, UK).

Geoff Page is based in Canberra and has published 25 collections of poetry as well as two novels and five verse novels. His recent books include *In medias res* (Pitt Street Poetry) and *101 Poems: 2012-2021* (Pitt Street Poetry). He reviews Australian poetry extensively and has run monthly poetry readings and jazz concerts in Canberra for many years.

Jean Page was born in Hobart and has lived in Lisbon, Portugal, with her family since 1997. A researcher, she participates in a local stanza group of the UK Poetry Society. She has published poetry in *Island* magazine. She lived in Canberra from 1979 to 1994.

Anita Patel is a Canberra writer. Her two collections of poetry are *Petals Fall* (Recent Work Press, 2022) and *A Common Garment* (Recent Work Press, 2019). Her work also appears in publications such as:

Mascara Literary Review, Cordite Poetry Review, Plumwood Mountain Journal and *Australian Poetry Anthology* Vol. 8.

Michael Sharkey has published many books, and taught, edited and reviewed poetry. His most recent book, *What If I Told You?— Unlikely Love Poems on Several Occasions* (Puncher and Wattmann) is a miscellany of 77 uncollected, mostly unpublished poems in casual fourteen-line verses, dating from 1965 until 2022.

Melinda Smith is a poet, editor, teacher, arts advocate and event curator based on Ngunnawal and Ngambri country. She is the author of seven poetry collections, including the 2014 Prime Minister's Literary Award-winner *Drag down to unlock or place an emergency call* (Pitt Street Poetry). Her latest books are *Goodbye, Cruel* (Pitt Street Poetry, 2017), the chapbook *Listen, bitch,* with artist Caren Florance (Recent Work Press, 2019) and *Man-handled* (Recent Work Press 2020).

Todd Turner is an Australian poet, and goldsmith. He has published two collections of poetry, *Woodsmoke* (Black Pepper Publishing) and *Thorn* (Puncher and Wattmann). His work is rooted in lived experience, and is noted for its precision and attention to visual detail. This is a poet who brings his work close to worship, who engages the large and small particulars of the world with intense resolve and clarity. He is working on a manuscript for his third collection, and is currently writing poems on the life of John Keats.

Kimberly K. Williams is the author of three books of poetry, *Still Lives* (Life Before Man, 2022), *Sometimes a Woman* (Recent Work Press, 2021) and *Finally, the Moon,* (Stephen F Austin State UP, 2017). *Still Lives* won a Canberra Critics Circle Award in Writing and was shortlisted for the ACT notable book of the year in poetry. Kimberly is from Detroit, Michigan.

www.ingramcontent.com/pod-product-compliance
Lightning Source LLC
Chambersburg PA
CBRC090837010526
44107CB00052B/1639